If Nothing Changes, Then Nothing Will Ever Change

By: Michael Zeidenberg

IF NOTHING CHANGES, NOTHING WILL EVER CHANGE Copyright © 2018 by Michael Zeidenberg. All rights are reserved. No part of this book may be used or reproduced in any manner whatsoever without written permission except in the case of brief quotations embodied in critical articles and reviews. For more information, address to Michael Zeidenberg at: michaelzeidenberg@gmail.com

FIRST EDITION

Photography and layout by Marla Zeidenberg
www.marlazeidenberg.com
Editing provided by Marnie G Ferguson of Note Editorial and Publishing Services   www.noteeditorialandpublishing.ca

This book is dedicated to my family who has provided me with inspiration, support and love. Without them and our journey together this book would not have been possible. I would also lIke to give special recognition to my son Brian who provided me with the initial inspiration to write this book.

Table of Contents

Introduction　　　　　　　　　　　　5

Part 1

Nothing Comes For Free　　　　　　12
Create a Positive Environment　　　17
Find a Mentor　　　　　　　　　　22
Choose the Right Business Partners　25
Stay the Course　　　　　　　　　30
Work the System　　　　　　　　　34
The Grass Is Not Always Greener　　37
Education Is Key　　　　　　　　　41
Abuse in the Workplace　　　　　　43
Learn to Listen　　　　　　　　　　47
Trust in Yourself and Focus on You　51
Live a Healthy Lifestyle　　　　　　57
Do What You Love　　　　　　　　59
Put Your Needs First　　　　　　　61
Don't Let Your Past Define You　　　63

Part Two

Goal Setting along with a Vision　　67
About the Author　　　　　　　　　81

Introduction

Imagine a life filled with happiness and prosperity. You are able to come and go as you please, purchase what you want when you want. You own a home with no mortgage; drive a nice car or maybe even two. You are able to take a vacation when you choose. You are able to live life to the fullest, a life that is far beyond your wildest dreams. You can spoil your family, treat your parents to trips, buy a car for a birthday gift, treat your kids to games, clothes...whatever their hearts desire.

Keep dreaming and make the dream grow. Nicer, bigger and better; more clothes, more jewellery, maybe a vacation home. Everything gets larger than life.

Now, take a moment and close your eyes and imagine your own life and dreams. Be patient with your thoughts make it as grand, fun and colourful as possible.

But then... Bang! It all tumbles down and you are left with nothing. You have lost your job or business. No house, no car, no money and more debt than you could ever imagine. So much debt that you are drowning in it. You can't seem to come up for air; there is no one there to save you. You can't seem to get anything to work in your favour. And you can't even find your mojo.

You are feeling lost, alone, and no one is there to listen to your thoughts, your deepest darkest secrets. Your friends seem to have all disappeared; they are suddenly nowhere to be found. Family members stop calling you. No one is checking in and asking how you are doing. No one is asking if they can do anything to help you. When they see you in the streets they seem to run from you as though in fear of catching the virus; the Bankruptcy Virus. Strong friendships and great partnerships — or at the very least business relationships; where are they now? Gone! Everyone you knew, partied with, worked with and simply enjoyed life with, are nowhere to be found.

You are alone.

You feel down and out, sadness overwhelms you and a grey cloud of depression is starting to materialize over your head. What do you do? You have a wife, kids and even a dog to look after.

In 1992 I went personally bankrupt and experienced all of these feelings. The financial trauma took a toll on my family. We had no money in the bank, a beautiful home that we no longer owned, cars that were returned to dealerships and our family was suddenly left penniless. My wife and I could not afford to go out for dinner; my kids could not go to school events because we could not afford to pay the costs for them to participate. Life felt impossible and the financial trauma unbearable. How on earth do you deal with the trauma of losing everything?

I was depressed, struggling with how to heal myself and wondering how I could ever recover from my financial trauma. I knew that if I did not do something to change my situation I would remain in a void and unable to create a strategy for my financial recovery.

It was a very dark time for me. I was in pain from my bankruptcy and was not sure how to move forward. But I realized if I did nothing than my life would remain empty.

It was my son Brian who helped me to see the light. He said, "Dad, writing a book about what you have gone through would be a great way to help heal yourself, as well as help others who may have gone through the same things. It may also be a great way to make some money, or it may help you figure out what you want to do next." My son's insightful statement helped stimulate my energy and put me on a path of recovery.

This is where the real story starts and the life lessons begin. My experiences span some thirty-five years of learning. I have experienced lots of joy, lots of pain and then lots of joy, and then more pain and back to the job — it's the way life works; like riding a roller coaster up and down and all around.

I hope you will learn from reading this book how to avoid some of the pitfalls I encountered and mistakes I made during my career, and more importantly you may find ways of preventing some of the downfalls I experienced. This book is about life lessons that can be used in business and in your personal life. You will also learn a method of setting goals and implementing plans that will help point you in a positive direction.

I have learned that it is important to know how to create an environment of positive change because...if nothing changes then nothing will ever change. This book is to help someone who has gone through crisis and how to recover. It will help them understand the need to reach out, view themselves from within and then how to grow and heal. The following lessons come out of the experience I had and I hope they will guide you on your path. They are lessons that apply to our lives but feel free to modify and create your own process after reading this book. Each of us is unique — what we learn may need to be modified for our own personal use.

There are two parts to the book. Part One includes the life lessons and some of my own experiences. Part Two is a ten-year plan for making real change in your personal, as well as your financial life.

PART ONE

Life Lesson Number 1

Nothing Comes For Free

Have you ever thought that some people are luckier than others? They have the Midas touch or that lucky charm that sits in their back pocket. Life provides some people a lot of abundance, and for some, more than they really need. Are you one of these people? I was not; I had to struggle and work for what I got.

However, appearances can be deceiving. These "lucky" people have usually had to pay something for their good fortune. Some may have worked very hard, put many hours into education and dedication to their life's work. Others may have used their smarts just when it was most critical to achieve their success. And some may have simply inherited their good fortune. But who knows what it cost them personally.

Nothing comes for free. Success always has a price. Usually, successful people had to either pay for their education and work hard, or for others success may have been achieved through the school of "hard knocks."

Learning through the school of hard knocks can be tough. It may not be obvious but many successful people have opened one or more businesses in their past, only to have lost them for any number of reasons — bankruptcy, competition, poor decision making, or even emotional setbacks.

We only gain experience by doing. We may win and we may lose, but the school of hard knocks teaches us what we need to know when moving forward to a new challenge. The key to this learning is much like a child learning to walk. When you fall down, just get back up. Fall again and get right back up again. Eventually we learn how to master how to walk, run and jump. In business, we learn the dos and don'ts of running a business through the same methodology.

Successful people used their hard-knocks education, which cost them time, money and emotional duress, to finally create their success story.

Every winner had to pay a price. Once you have accepted this fact, feelings of jealousy or contempt for others will disappear from your life. You learn to be happy for other people's success. You learn to enjoy their happiness and good fortune because now you realize that like them, your success is up to you and no one else. They paid their price for success because it did not come for free. Learning from successful people can be powerful and rewarding.

It's a funny thing success; success prefers to hang out with folks that enjoy or have developed their own success. It also seems to rub off on others or flows like a river from one lake to another. But you have to be in the water to feel and embrace that sensation.

So, let me first share an experience I had of hanging out with "successful" people. I was part of a group of entrepreneurs and we had each created our own abundance of wealth. We got into some investments together and became close friends — or so I believed at the time. I travelled and spent money as they did, trying to keep up (yes, with the Jones's).

One year the group of us went to Las Vegas. I remember eating in a very nice restaurant called The Pamplemousse. It was at the end of a day of gambling and shopping and we were loud, obnoxious and very rude. We were drinking and eating like the ultra-wealthy who did not have a concern in the world, the nouveaux riche who just don't care about anyone around them. We were having a great time and we got louder and louder until it reached a point where we were affecting everyone else in the restaurant. As long as we were having a good time, who cared about anyone around us? Eventually, the management asked us to leave. This was just not cool and frankly, something that today I would never do.

I thought at the time, that by hanging out with these wealthy people, who I thought were my friends, I could grow my wealth. And I did for a period of time, until one of the deals went sour. The friendships started to crumble. And today there is only one person from that group that I still remain friends with. I confess that during that time I felt I was on top of the world and that nothing could take me down. Wow, was I surprised.

These types of groups and situations can make you feel like part of a private members club. But there is a flip side to hanging out with some successful people. You can learn from them what made them successful and how you can emulate that success for yourself. But the question remains, are they really friends?

Life Lesson Number 2

Create a Positive Environment

What avenues are available to create a new and stronger network of friends and business associates? Religious organizations — a church, synagogue, mosque, or temple; sports teams and clubs, networking groups such as a Business Network International (BNI) or professional business groups such as Presidents of Enterprising Organizations (PEO), TEC Canada or your local Chamber of Commerce.

While it is very important to get out and meet people, it is also important to get online with social media. LinkedIn has provided me with a wealth of connections. If you are shy or uncomfortable with meeting new people face-to-face at networking events, then LinkedIn is a wonderful way to test the waters and ask others for advice or input. There are many people who will share their thoughts and are open to helping others. Invite them to join your network.

You can also join specialized networking groups that match your expertise and background. LinkedIn has a variety of interest groups that may tie into your background, expertise or education. LinkedIn is a great platform to create a network of people that you can connect with, talk to and learn from.

You can also enrol in one or two courses to help upgrade your skills or simply keep yourself engaged within a positive environment. Balance the need of looking after problems with the need of directing your mind towards the positive. Education is a positive no matter what your interests are.

Another method of creating a strong and supportive network of people which worked wonders for me was my Mastermind Group. Think of three or four people you know or have been associated with that you admire and who inspire you. Invite them to form a group called My Mastermind Group.

Mastermind groups have been around for many years. The members of the group provide different skills and strengths. Each one brings a complement of strengths, interests, resources and views that can help and support all the members. It's a fantastic place for sharing intimate and private thoughts. Members do not criticize but share their thoughts in a constructive and supportive manner. They do not judge. It is a blessing to be part of such a group that can help when you feel there is no one else out there for you, other than your immediate family. It is a place to bounce ideas off of one another or simply brainstorm. You will be amazed what can be created out of being part of a mastermind group. Many unique and interesting ideas have been forged by these types of relationships.

Finally, donating some time to a charitable organization can provide many benefits. It will help your networking and fill your days. You will feel happy and positive because you are making a positive contribution and helping others. It's a great motivator and it's a "win–win" — you are helping others while you help yourself.

In the end, one or all of these approaches will help create a new and fresh network which will help you turn your situation around. You can never have too many venues for networking.

Also, most of these activities are free. If you form a mastermind group you can meet at members' homes, or in a public place. Social media is free as is going to your spiritual place of worship. You just need to look around and assess the economics of what you need to do and determine how much money you are prepared to spend to create this new network. As an example joining a BNI group usually costs a few dollars for attending a meeting plus your breakfast. The total cost could be under $25.00.

If you do nothing to change, then nothing will ever change… but if you work on changing things up, things will change. You have nothing to lose and everything to gain. So take the time and list the venues that you think may work best for you and start taking those first steps into the world of networking, and create those new friends and business relations. Those folks will become supportive friends, new sources of referrals and may have connections that can help with the creation of a new and successful path.

Life Lesson 3

Find a Mentor

Our parents are our original life coaches. But successful friends, family and business associates can also help you with success. Among them you can find your life coach or mentor.

Learning how to behave and think like your mentor or mentors is a way of developing a successful outlook and a positive view of life. But you may ask, "How the heck do I meet these new friends and business associates? Better yet, how do I ask them to be my coach or mentor?"

Great questions, and to answer them we go back to the basics. How did you choose your other friends and business associates? Or, did they choose you? And, ask yourself why, in both cases. It's important to know this, as it will help you choose your new friends and associates differently. A good idea is to make up a list of questions to help create the clarity needed when selecting these folks. Here are some questions you may want to ask yourself.

Do I like this person and do I enjoy hanging out with them?

Is this person open and genial?

Do I respect what this person stands for?

Do they have the honesty and integrity I'm looking for?

Do I find them interesting and do I want to be like them?

What are some of their attributes that attract me to them?

If you have positive responses to these questions when considering a person, they may be a good choice for making a new friend.

If you are married or in a relationship, your first course of action could be to seek out your partner's counsel. You could also talk to a parent, relative or even one of your children, but you cannot afford to be shy or afraid to engage in a dialogue with them. It will amaze you how wise they are. They feel your pain; because they are family and the conversation is easy, and they understand what you are going through because they are there with you. Sometimes we don't really appreciate those who are really in our corner.

Life Lesson Number 4

Choose the Right Business Partners

The worst experience I ever had, and the hardest lesson I have learned is when I had to claim personal bankruptcy. Not only did I lose my wife's and my own life savings, but we lost our house, and I put my kids' futures at risk. It also negatively affected family relations whereby my wife's family sued me.

"How did this happen?" you may ask in wonder. At the time we were involved in a number of investments that required me to be the front man. Prior to my insolvency, I knew I needed to divest myself of those investments. So, I transferred ownership of the investments to them (for one dollar), as I was not able to pay the monthly costs. Yup, that's how it worked...my wife's family (excluding one brother) got my share of the investments for free and then they sued me because they now had to make the monthly payments. The investments still provided huge tax benefits for each of them and they earned a fantastic return on them.

So this life lesson is to avoid partnerships with family members unless you have legal agreements in place. We never know what life may bring us and there will be times we need an exit strategy that works, thus an agreement drawn up by a lawyer that outlines the business relationship as well as the exit strategy is a must.

Creating a contract flows right into the decision whether to partner with family members or not. While partnering with my in-laws had its pitfalls, my parents did one better. They were not wealthy people, yet they guaranteed a loan so that my wife and I could get into a franchised business. From the people who had the least financially I got the most support. My folks offered their time, energy, love, and spiritual support. They were willing to do everything in their power to help us and with no strings attached.

Know who is in your corner. We learned that we have family that love us and will support us at any cost or risk. When things go well, we never have an issue. When things don't go well... look out. As in any partnership make sure there is a legal agreement in place. Agreements protect all the parties concerned whether they are family, friends or business partners. An agreement also helps define everyone's responsibilities and it provides an exit strategy. Thus the life lesson, know who is in your corner and make it legal.

If going into business with a family member is not an option, how do you choose a business partner? My first experience with a partnership was with a group of friends investing in homes to renovate and sell. My second partnership was in a construction company with a long-time friend. My third business partnership was with a trusted friend — I had known Rick for most of my life; we became partners in a franchise business.

In any partnership it is important to understand the dynamics of the relationship between the partners.

Typically, we tend not to understand the value of each other's strengths and weaknesses, dedication and energy. Once we have entered the partnership it's only then that we start to understand what we are looking for in each other to support the business. There can be a level of jealousy or we may start to question the effort put into the business by each person. These types of issues can negatively affect the working relationship.

The key to these relationships is to establish clear job descriptions and responsibilities, and who has the final say. I recommend putting in place a working agreement prior to the start of the partnership, as this will help everyone understand each person's roles and responsibilities. It will also eliminate most of the day-to-day issues that may arise between business partners.

Life lesson, when entering into partnerships prepare an agreement that both parties understand and agree to. As part of the working agreement you may want to prepare an exit strategy for all partners concerned. Once again, this will eliminate many issues should there be a falling out between the partners.

Life Lesson Number 5

Stay the Course

As a young man starting out, I did not really know what I wanted out of life. After high school I went to Ryerson University and took business. I was an average student but I knew one thing — I wanted to be in business. I wanted what my relatives and some friends possessed a business that provided a lifestyle of abundance and wealth. I liked the thought of being able to wheel and deal (negotiate); it seemed like fun.

So, I went to business school and learned the ins and outs of business. After I graduated I realized I needed more education so I entered the CMA (Certified Management Accounting) program. Without certification I could not get a job with an accounting firm, which was the only way to become a Chartered Accountant in those days and learn more about business. Now, when I look back, I realize that this was a strange approach to getting into a business because really, I wanted to be an entrepreneur — I wanted to own my own business. But I had no idea what my passions were and no money to invest. I had no idea what kind of business I wanted to be involved with.

Today I am still trying to figure out what kind of business interests me. Here is what I do know about myself.

I am an idealist. I believe you need to give back in order to receive. I have strong convictions about recycling and leaving the environment a better place for future generations. I enjoy constructing things, specifically houses, roadways and environmental settings such as hardscapes — leaving my mark in the world. I'm not an egotistical person but I have a type "A" personality, so I enjoy directing and influencing others; solving problems and supporting others. I am the happiest when I see that my help has allowed others to do well and succeed in their personal and professional lives. It's my way of giving back.

I enjoy hard work, mental and physical. I love solution-based selling, especially when it is "one-on-one" selling. I believe the customer comes first and I am great at providing superior customer service. I have learned that this is something some businesses do not do well.

Over the course of my career I changed jobs rather frequently, typically every two or three years. I would end up leaving one company for another, sometimes because of office politics.

I have learned that I don't enjoy playing politics in the business world. For example, groups of team members or senior management who try to get an influential individual to join a side in a dispute, without regard for what is best for business. These power struggles create a negative work environment, which affects how the company operates and makes decisions. I believe that team members and management only need one team. Team ONE that drives sales, profits and creates a positive work environment for all members.

I recommend looking for job opportunities that allow for career growth. Being mobile and willing to move positions within the company will help to instill employment stability, and provide insight into different areas of the business, which will allow for educational growth as well as career development.

Looking back I see a career-minded executive trying to force his career advancement. I was not a patient person, so I jumped at the next opportunity for career growth. Some would say I never paid my dues, but I did. I helped create many success stories while advancing my career. However, if I were asked advice today about how to grow and develop a career, I would say, "Stay the course." Put in the time and establish tenure with that choice company. Today's business environment is very challenging and many companies are prepared to invest in their human capital... that's you!

Life Lesson Number 6

Work the System

To grow your career you need to continue enhancing your education as well as getting relevant work experience.

Once you have found that company of choice, take your time and work the system. Learn the company's system of creating careers for employees within the organization, work on enhancing your business network as well as your support groups, and develop your brand. Your brand is a way of distinguishing yourself from others, which helps you stand out from the others or who you may be competing against for a new role. Which phone manufacturer seems to have the best name in the marketplace? Many of you would say "Apple." That's a brand that stands out. In the same way your personal brand is about how you stand out against everyone else.

It's hard to job jump. Be patient with your role, your boss and the company. Find that special coach or mentor to help with your growth and advancement. It will take place if you are prepared to pay the price…ah, the catch phrase "pay the price." The price is the time and effort required to obtain your goal or goals. Education, hard work, a network of support and managing your patience will bring you closer to success. Career development does not happen overnight, it takes a strategy. Create the plan, put in the time and effort and your rewards will come. Strategy and planning are about sitting down and plotting out what is required to get to where you need to go. For example, if your long-term goal is to be a Chief Financial Officer you may need to review what you already have and what you need:

First, make sure you have completed your formal training.

Second, obtain the best accounting job you can land and start gaining relevant business experience.

Third, find a mentor who can coach you on how best to develop your skills and network.

Fourth, determine timelines that may be necessary to move through the different accounting roles. For example, you may plan to be an accounting clerk for two years, an accountant for two years and a controller for five years and eventually move into a Chief Financial Officers role.

Yes, the key to a successful professional career is to work the system, don't give up easily and go through the steps of creating a successful plan. I'd say to my kids, avoid getting frustrated, continue to stay focused and find a mentor or group that can help you continue to grow and be nurtured from within.

Life Lesson Number 7

The Grass Is Not Always Greener

I moved from company to company until I found a home with a family-based construction company. Due to my work history, my accounting and management skills were very strong. Even though I had not completed my accounting designation I was still able to achieve many accomplishments. I jumped into this company with my heart and soul only to learn within my first two months that the company was insolvent, virtually on the verge of bankruptcy. I had a new question. Do I bail and run for the hills or do I dig in my heels and stay the course?

Lucky for me I decided to stay the course. I worked crazy hours and would wake up in the middle of the night with an idea of how best to solve a problem. My wife was not too excited about these "midnight wake-up calls," but she put up with them. Next to my bed I kept a paper and pen on my nightstand so I could quickly jot down those thoughts because I knew if I ignored my ideas they would be lost to the night. Those midnight dreams produced my most unique thoughts, which allowed me to solve numerous operating issues.

I quickly realized that it did not matter how tired I was, I needed to find more ways to continue that creativity. This process has taken some time to learn — more than thirty-five years to learn a variety of ways of being creative.

Here are some methods to help your mind maintain its creativity.

First be well rested, eat healthy foods, and exercise. Yes this sounds like a diet and it's true! Being healthy and fit will allow you and your mind to be in a positive state. The mind does not like to be told what to do. If it is starving for the necessities of life it will react in a negative way. It also likes to be used; reading, learning, and challenging one's mind keeps it sharp and ready for work. I have also learned that the mind enjoys the quiet. Meditation, quieting the mind and clearing the noise of the day helps the mind to be creative. I meditate on a daily basis. I have found over the years that using positive words, affirmations and phrases help keep my mind, body and soul positive and they help me maintain happy thoughts. I also post daily inspirational thoughts online. This process sets the stage for a day filled with creativity, thoughtfulness, positivity and success.

After almost a decade working for this company whose success I was instrumental in driving, I started to gain confidence — way too much confidence, to the point where I got cocky about my strengths and I became arrogant. I tried to gain more wealth by asking for shares in the family's new business ventures. When one too many no's were tossed my way (bearing in mind I was paid exceptionally well and saving most of my income), I got frustrated and left. I bought into my friend's construction company who happened to be one of our subcontractors. Within three years the company I bought into went into bankruptcy and I personally went bankrupt the following year.

I now see that leaving the company I worked for was absolutely the worst decision I ever made. I forgot about being patient. Had I stayed the course and not thought my life was so bad, my financial affairs would have fared much better. The lesson was simple; the grass is not always greener on the other side. In fact, I did not appreciate what I had. I did not realize that my income was far better than what the construction market could offer nor could I foresee the financial exposure that lay ahead when I acquired joint ownership of the construction company. I did not have to jump ship to find out I could grow my own green grass where I was. I had gained much wealth through my savings and investments. My grass was full and lush.

Life Lesson Number 8

Education Is Key

At all costs, make sure you get an education, no matter what! And, continue your educational growth. It does not have to involve structured classes, but specializing in an industry and enrolling in programs or courses within it will help advance your career. And remember to keep track of the courses you complete. They will have a huge value because they provide accountability and validation of your knowledge. Improving your skills and knowledge through education will also help you to develop your network, because of the new relationships that you will develop while in the classroom environment.

As I said earlier, I was in the CMA program, got to the fifth level and then I had to write my last exam. I wrote the exam but I failed. Worse, I ran out of time to complete the program. Instead of fighting to get my accounting designation by reapplying and repeating the last three courses in the fifth level, I took what I thought was the easy way out and focused on my career.

I moved around a lot. I worked on the road as an Operational Auditor for Rio Algom, a worldwide mining company. This was my third job. I also had just gotten married and my wife was pregnant with our first baby. Instead of staying the course with this company, I jumped. But in this case, I left because I did not want to be away from my wife and baby and my job meant a lot of time spent on the road.

Early in my career I thought I could get away without obtaining a CMA, but today I realize it was a huge mistake to not finish the program. The accounting designation would have made advancing my career easier and provided more opportunities. It would have improved my credibility and opened many more doors more easily. Bottom line; finish what you start especially when it comes to your formal education.

Life Lesson Number 9

Abuse in the Workplace

There are always ups and downs in our work relationships; however abuse, verbal or physical, is not an acceptable practice anywhere and should not be tolerated. Yet, it becomes far more challenging when we are confronted by abuse in the workplace. We are afraid of losing our job if we respond or fight back.

I've experienced verbal and physical abuse while working in two different organizations. The first time, I experienced verbal threats from other senior management leaders who asked to meet me offsite. Five VPs met me in a hotel conference room and basically cornered me. They said that I was to either fall in line or accept the consequences. The meaning of "consequences" was left to my imagination, but I interpreted it to mean either physical abuse or they would make sure my remaining days at this company would be horrific. At the time, I was the company's Chief Financial Officer and had a fair bit of clout within and outside of the organization. In the end, I was dismissed by the president because I would not conform to his unethical decision on how to manage an exit strategy for his partner, who was also his brother.

The second situation was similar to a love-hate relationship. Initially I had a very strong working relationship with the owner; he relied on and trusted me as I was brought in as his financial confidant. Everything ran smoothly for a period of time — we had a fantastic working relationship — until one day there was a massive power outage affecting the Southern Ontario Region. Friday August 14, 2003 just after 4:00 p.m. the power went out. The business where I worked was located an hour-and-a-half drive by car, on a good day, from my home. At 4:30 that day, I left and headed home. The drive took me almost five hours because of the power outage, the traffic and, to make matters worse, my gas tank was on empty. I was running on fumes when I pulled into my driveway.

The company barbecue happened to be on that weekend. Unfortunately, the power had not yet been restored where I lived, but it was in Hamilton, where the company was located. As it turned out I missed that barbecue because there was no power in our area so I was unable to fill the gas tank in my car. I wasn't going anywhere that day. Monday morning I was not greeted well. The owner and his family members treated me terribly. I understood that as the Chief Operating Officer I was expected to have been there. But my explanation of the situation fell on deaf ears.

From that point forward I had a love-hate relationship with the owner. The verbal abuse started and eventually that verbal abuse morphed into a physical form. The owner would punch me in the shoulder or body check me into the wall. Being knocked around was not welcomed, yet I still needed the job. The relations continued to deteriorate until both parties came to the conclusion that parting ways was the best choice.

No one should have to put up with any abuse in the workplace. I have particular concerns with small and mid-size companies that do not have a human resources department or adequate workplace safety policies in place. Employees are faced with a number of challenges. If they experience abuse, should they stay in their position, take the abuse and not say anything, and work towards gaining the respect that might stop the abuse? Should they go to the labour board and file a complaint, or should they simply find a new job and leave?

This life lesson is to never tolerate abuse. Deal with the abuser head on, but if all else fails it's best to just leave. Life is too short to deal with negativity in the workplace. It pulls us down to a level where it affects our mindset. I would always give up the negativity, even for a lower paid job that offered a positive and friendly work environment.

Life Lesson Number 10

Learn to Listen

In my position with the family-run construction company, I started to give of myself, by putting in more personal time and energy that went beyond the standard workday. A little self-sacrifice allowed me to join the senior management team and owner in the overall management of the company. My efforts were well rewarded; over the years the company grew from insolvency to the second largest contractor in its sector. The instrumental change happened during that time. Gino, the father who owned the company liked me. He took me under his wing and taught me the business. This was when I learned it was better not to talk but to listen. Learning to listen allowed me to learn from him and with that I found my first business mentor.

Gino and I developed a great friendship. He was patient and took his time teaching me the business literally from the ground up. We would go to job sites together where he would explain the process and show me issues and flaws that were not represented in the construction drawings. From the site, we would go back to the office and on the formal construction drawings he would sketch in the amount of work completed and compare this to what he thought would have been completed, and thus determine whether production was on or off target. The variance of on-site progress would determine how he would strategize the next phase of work. Then, he would outline where possible issues were in the drawings (based on our site visits) and he would review the engineers' reports as well as any issues that came up at the job site.

He was always thinking outside of the box. Using the information on hand he would modify the plan and improve the efficiency of the installation, thus improving the job's profitability.

I knew by then to listen, digest, learn and ask questions when I needed to. It's important to note that this man did not have a high school education and English was his second language yet he was a brilliant man.

One of the key takeaways from this relationship was that every business should be built with four pillars. Not many businesses can rely on one business strength or one revenue stream. With only one source of income the business would be at risk should the company lose that one client. However, having a minimum of four major clients minimizes risk. If one leaves there are still have three major revenue channels. So, if we lose one leg or one sales channel we would still have three legs to stand on. Lose another we can still stand on two legs, but finally if we are left with only one leg, we had better be good at balancing and we had better make sure we are really strong because that one leg will need to stand the endurance of time.

This idea also remains consistent with a variety of different areas within a business. For example, we can look at teams within departments of a company. A team leader may be a vice president and that VP may have three directors reporting to them and each director may have three or four managers reporting to them. The key is to have someone in the lower tier ready and willing to take over the senior role when called up to action. The Pillar concept is in play even in an organizational chart.

The bottom line is, in business we should make sure we have more than one pillar and do not rely on only one leg. It's ideal to focus on a minimum of four pillars. Successful businesses require constant change. We must embrace change as part of any business, its culture and its daily operations.

Life Lesson Number 11

Trust in Yourself and Focus on You

So, after a life crisis, how do we get back on the horse? We are bumped, bruised, frustrated, tearful, fearful of what may happen, concerned about where the next dollar will come from and all that negative stuff. The fact is, when there is a will there is a way.

There will be moments when we will not be motivated and we need to find that mojo. This typically happens when we feel we have hit rock bottom. We soon understand that there is nowhere else to go but up. At some point we realize it's there. Slowly the motivation will kick in and that's when we decide to simply stand up and start the process. By starting "the doing," we recreate and nurture our motivation. Never, but never lie down and give up. Our mind's focus should be "we cannot give up."

As we start to step forward we will see minor wins. For example, our minds will suggest we make a few phone calls to start the networking process. We will be a little nervous making the first two or three calls and then we start to get into the swing of the process. We gain a bit of confidence and momentum with those calls, until one hits the mark. We have someone who is prepared to meet and chat. This feels like a win; we have started the process of creating some success, which feeds the motivation to push us forward with more eagerness. We start to want those successes and so we work even harder. It is beneath us to ever give up. We should always keep swinging the bat until we hit the homerun for the win.

As I have said, it starts with the mind, the body and then the soul.

I have a process that I have developed and fine-tuned over time. Through my experience I have learned a number of techniques from others and here is what I use.

First, I meditate. This lets the mind refocus or go through a reset. I find a quiet room or depending on weather I use the outdoors. I either sit in a relaxed position or lie down on my back with my legs bent and resting on the seat of a chair. I close my eyes and focus on my breathing, smooth, steady and deep breaths that flush out any tension I may be holding in. I listen to each breath flowing in and out and paying attention to each breath I begin to slow my breathing. I feel my body relax. I start with my head, clearing my thoughts and imagining each part of my body starting to relax.

The key is to always focus on releasing the tension. I will move from my head to my neck and shoulders continuing to flow to my arms and then move over to my upper body straight down to my lower back, my hips and then my legs and toes. My entire body becomes relaxed and tension-free. At some point my subconscious reaches a position where I can refocus my mind. It's that moment when I start to clear the noise out of my head removing each thought as it enters.

Once I have cleared the noise, I build a house with a safe room. The room is my quiet room. It has a door, windows and provides total protection from anything that could possibly harm me. I then start to see in my mind the image of my safe room. I walk into the room and I know I have built the room to my personal specifications. I like a bright room filled with the warmth of the sun, but the ambiance of the night air with the full moon and stars shining bright on me. Yes it sounds strange to have both the power of the day and the stillness of the night all in the same place. But this is my safe room and I can build it any way I see fit. As you will. Once in this room, I'm able to develop a deep meditative state.

I am able to go back to this room each day, where I feel safe and able to clear my mind and allow for the clarity of thought to commence. Ideas are created, patterns and direction are imagined and finally clarity is defined. I use this time to heal myself, redirect myself, help understand what, why, where, when or how things occur. It helps me to define me. It helps me explain to myself who I am and most importantly it helps to motivate me.

Mind healing can be done in many other ways, but this works best for me. I come out of it refreshed, motivated and ready to take on the world with a winning attitude!

Step two is to motivate my body. Yes, the E word...Exercise! We cannot move forward with just a great mind, we need a healthy body. Exercise can start off with swimming some laps, walking around the block, jogging, weight lifting, cycling or anything you enjoy that also makes you sweat. Don't choose something that you will not enjoy. Try everything until you find the one or two sports or exercises that help you be happy. It's got to be fun otherwise it will not work.

Nurturing the soul requires good conversation with friends, relatives and business associates. Reading a book, doing research, donating your time for a cause, taking up a challenge, helping out someone in need or simply applying steps one and two as part of your regular day will help feed the soul. The soul knows when it's thirsty and it needs to be monitored and more importantly it needs to be fed on a regular basis.

So, you may wonder how this is going to help you get back your mojo. This is about putting trust in you. Put that effort in and I assure you that your mojo will be back better than ever. You will have new strength, insight and ability to take those unknown steps, which will provide you with a bright future — because if nothing changes, nothing will ever change. I assure you ...you just changed if you did all this work!

Life Lesson Number 12

Live a Healthy Lifestyle

When your body, mind and soul are in a positive state you will find the network, people, answers and solutions you need more easily.

If you do not know the answer, you will figure it out and if you cannot figure it out, ask for help. There is always a way of finding a solution. So, eating right, exercising your body as well as your mind will certainly help steer you in the right direction. Healthy eating and exercise will help make you feel better physically while reading will help provide a bit more confidence given the added value of knowledge. The combination of these three will help reduce some of the stress you may be going through. Finally, if anything, the workouts and eating right provide the physical strength to fight the fight, because if nothing changes then nothing will ever change!

So, the life lesson here is healthy living helps keep the mind positive. The more positive we are the better we are equipped to manage stress and negativity. More importantly, the positive energy allows for the creativity and creativity helps attract positive and creative people — similar to success attracting success.

Life Lesson Number 13

Do What You Love

One of the greatest lessons I've learned is to find what makes you happy, that passion in life that helps you get up in the morning pumped and eager to go to work.

After many years I found my passion for coaching and mentoring. I love working with companies and family businesses on their strategic and succession plans; helping them customize the tools to manage, and grow their business.

Since leaving what I thought was my lifelong dream job, I finally found my passion — helping other entrepreneurs and senior managers grow and manage their business. I've worked with a number of small and mid-size companies and realized it took all my years of experience and education to reach a point where I can honestly say I'm there.

The bottom line is to embrace the change, because if nothing changes, then nothing will ever change.

Life Lesson Number 14

Put Your Needs First

This is an interesting lesson and has been a tough lesson for me. It's about putting "me" first. I'm still learning how I can control my inner feelings to be able to put my needs ahead of everyone else's needs. It's the theme of "survival of the fittest." It's much easier when the topic is a non-emotional connection. When family is involved, I have a very tough time putting myself first. I'm more concerned with my family then myself. I'm concerned about protecting them and ensuring their well-being to a point where I put their well-being above my own. That may come from being the head of the family.

The decision to put myself first is being selfish, but it is also about self-preservation. I cannot help anyone if I'm not strong and fit. Only the strong can be in a position to help others. It's as if we were all on a life raft, but there are not enough life jackets to go around. But the others feel they should just sit it out and wait. You are the strongest swimmer and can see the shore. If it were me I would take the life jacket and swim to shore. Saving myself first would allow me to save everyone else.

Life Lesson 15

Don't Let Your Past Define You

My next life lesson is a very sad story, but one of inspiration, healing and understanding the imbalance of the cycle of life.

A number of years ago a client of mine lost his son in a skateboarding accident. This loving dad, whose first wife had left him with two young kids, then went through a divorce with his second wife, and then had to make the decision to turn off his son's life support. And at the same time his business was falling into insolvency. He had so many negative issues beating on him. He was in terrible pain and was at the bottom of his world, yet somehow he made it back to the real world.

None of us could or would want to imagine losing a child. It is not part of the natural human life cycle. It is impossible to compare any experience we could have in life to losing a child. Yet this man worked his way out of a very negative and sad time and decided he was not going to let the loss of his son define his world. He was going to define his own world and decided to enrich to his daily activities by talking about his son. He was going to focus on a happy life not in spite of, but in light of his son's memory.

The way back starts with crying. And we cry a lot. Once the tears dry up, there is sadness, despair and loss. It's then we need to reach out for help. It will take time, energy and a desire to heal but we will get there. After such a loss it's up to us to live on to give meaning to that lost life. Despite our challenges and losses we cannot let them define who we are.

Many of us have periods in our lives that seem impossible to recover from. I know people who are at the bottom of their world because of divorce, bankruptcy, loss of jobs or friends.

We have no right to compare, but if a dad can bounce back and embrace and enjoy a life again after he lost his child, there is absolutely no reason we could not be inspired and decide to lead a happier life regardless of our own situations and hardships. We should never let the past define who we are, but we can let the past allow us to define who we want to be, a positive, happy, fulfilled and loving person.

What I've learned is that no matter how bad life can be we can recover from it and still live a happy and successful life. But it's up to us, and no one else, to make that choice. If someone can come back from such personal trauma, I believe that many of us can come back from a bankruptcy or making poor life choices. We can come back from anything if we choose to. Why, because if nothing changes then nothing will ever change.

PART TWO

Life Lesson 16

Goal Setting along with a Vision

It's amazing all the lessons we learn during our lifetime. The question is, did we really learn from our education? Did I learn enough to be able to put what I learned into practice? I realize now that a major life lesson was how to create a detailed plan that drilled down into the nitty-gritty. I needed to itemize steps and fill in the detail. I should have had a clear vision and been able to put it down on paper. In the past I may have "talked the talk" but I did a poor job "walking the talk," and my wife Marla agrees with this statement.

So, here is my final life lesson — how to make that plan.

The plan is about setting goals and timelines that we can achieve. We start with something simple and achievable. Once we create consistency we can build on it. Something simple and something that would take no more than a minute or two each day, such as setting a goal to do five push ups every day. When you feel that it's time, build on the five and make it six, then seven, until you decide that you can do ten push ups every day. It all starts with setting goals that we can achieve. It builds our confidence and as we become more confident we learn to build on what we have achieved.

This journey is focused on creating and achieving your long-term goals. It starts with a process like this and by answering some questions. Your responses to these questions will help you understand why you need a strategy or process and what your game plan will be to develop the strategy. So, let's start by taking out a pen and paper or your laptop or tablet and answer the following questions:

Am I happy with the state of my life and career?

Am I performing as well as I possibly can?

Do I need to revise how I present myself to the world? Is this the best image I can create for myself?

Will measuring how well I achieved my past goals, help me achieve a new set of goals for this coming year?

Are you prepared to make modification to your life to accomplish your new goals?

What are the risks if I don't set new aspirations for the year?

Does economics play a role in the planning and decision-making process for this year or next? If so, how does it and why?

Do I have time to work on this process? If not, why?

If time is an issue how can I create the time necessary to complete these goals?

In order to achieve my goals, do I need more resources such as training, coaching, education, mentoring or equipment?

Once you have answered these questions you should be ready and willing to create the time and energy to work on this process. Once you have decided you are ready to move forward, you will need to create an environment where you can be creative and start thinking "outside of the box." Many people start the process in a place where they feel happy and can have freedom to think. It may be a coffee shop, a beach or park; it could be over a beer, a glass of wine at the cottage or sitting in front of a roaring fire. Typically this process is not done in the office and cell phones should be turned off! Some people may even enjoy listening to music while engaged in this process.

It's time to take action. So once again, grab that same pad of paper or computer and on **a** blank page list a win or a loss and continue listing your wins and losses of the past year on separate page. For those goals that were wins, rate each goal from one to ten. For those goals that have a rating of less than seven decide whether you want to keep them on your new goal list. If so, list them on a third page.

Now review the list of losses. Are there any goals on that list you feel should be added to your new goal list? If so, add them to the list. Now we have a starting point. Add to the list any additional goals for the coming year that come to mind. Commence the thought process. Do not rush through this process, as it is very important to understand what you are focusing on.

Now that you are queued up, it's time to start generating those creative "out of the box" thoughts. Now start jotting down your ideas. The process is that simple! The key is to feel free to have unencumbered thoughts. Your goals can be short-term and long-term. No thought is a bad thought! No goal is a bad goal!

Once you have established your goals move on to the next stage of the process by following the next eight steps:

Step One

Focus on where you would like to be in ten years. Create a vision that makes you feel happy and successful. Now that you have that picture, start to list your expected life achievements. Your list can be as simple or complex as you desire. It could include the type of job you have or the type of business you own or, if you already own a business, it may be about creating its own achievements. You could include what you live in and where and how much wealth you have.

Step Two

Now, list your top ten goals by priority — they can be personal or professional. (If you have more than ten goals then feel free to list them all.) The most important should be first and so on down the line. Add details and information about each goal. For example, if you are considering purchasing a home, try describing it. A house or a condo, the number of bedrooms, square footage, how many fireplaces and where they may be located. If it is a job, write down the type of job, what your earnings would be and follow the same process for each vision. Don't forget to include goals that you kept from the past list.

Step Three

This where the process starts to get interesting: Think about what you need to do in the next three and five years in order to achieve your ten-year desires. Write down for each of these periods what your life looks like and what you will need to do to make that ten-year vision a reality. What will be your successes and more importantly what do you need to do and learn in order to achieve your goals? Can you describe your personality? Are you friendly, driven, interactive with the people around you, are you fun loving? What is your lifestyle? Can you describe the type of friends and business associates you have and do they spiritually (or financially) support you or do you help them? Does your mind, body and soul match theirs or at least partially? It is important to describe the above in as much detail as possible for the three and five-year time periods. Note: You should reference the steps in years three and five that refer to your wishes for your ten-year plan. The objective is to understand what we are doing in year three and five that helps achieve the goals for the ten-year plan.

Step Four

List the resources — people, training and education, equipment, coaches and experience — you will need to achieve those changes in the three and five year periods. You may also want to list what your yearly needs are starting from year one and work up to year ten.

Step Five

Now we look at the money management and financial well-being of your goal setting. On a separate piece of paper list all of your current expenses. List all the expenses and payments that you incur including what leaves your pocket (and bank account) from daily coffee to your mortgage and car payments. Annualize your total spending. Based on those numbers take a serious look at what can be done to reduce the cash outflow. Can you replace your desires with something a bit less expensive? Can you reduce your annual insurance costs? Can you modify your mortgage or line of credit? How are we managing those credit cards? Do they need to be consolidated or better yet how can the monthly payments disappear?

If you need help, there are many excellent financial planners that can assist you. If you prefer to continue to manage the process yourself, then try this. The objective is to pay yourself first, but you need to be in a position to do that. So let's try to implement the 1% rate reduction rule. For every cost component that you have, try to reduce the cost or improve the efficiency of that cost burden by 1%. Go back to the spending list you prepared and review your spending patterns. Now, instead of 1% let's make our target 2.5%. For example, can you reduce the cost of your mobile phone expenses by 2.5%? Or how can you reduce your groceries by 2.5%?

To help you reduce expenses develop some steps to follow that will help you manage your money. Try to list as many ideas as possible. Then work on how to create the steps and procedures to achieve each cost reducing goal that is on your list. You may see some items on your list that you could save more than 2.5%, so those are the first action steps to be taken.

As part of the financial planning process, you may want to also consider the revenue side. Earning more income may mean finding a new job or a second job, or meeting with a financial planner to review any investments you may have. If you don't have any, it might be time to include creating an investment portfolio in your plans. Based on your plan, you may have a dollar value assigned to savings. Using some of this you could start an investment plan. Wow, we have just created a way of you to starting to pay yourself first!

A financial planner or accountant may be able to fine tune the process and inform you of other opportunities to improve your financial well-being such as tax planning.

Step Six

It is time to review the overall vision you have created for your ten period. Get a very clear picture and write down five action items for each timeline — in year three and year five — that you would need to achieve your vision for year ten. Next, list five action items for the next twelve months for each goal of your new plan. Attach timelines and resources to each action.

Step Seven

Keep yourself accountable by reviewing your progress each week. Enter your steps into a calendar and then review the time targets that were set out. Your goals will never be achieved if they are not reviewed regularly. Review your plan annually. Make any modifications as needed to accommodate any changes to your life over the year. If you have trouble doing it alone, try sharing the responsibility with a partner, friend or spouse.

Step Eight

Finally, I recommend that you set goals for the well-being of your mind, body and soul's well-being in addition to those for your financial well-being.

You now have the tools to create a pathway to what you really desire in life. You have many life lessons to learn and many twists and turns to experience during your lifetime. The key is to never give up. We may fall down, but we must get back up. We will have losses and we will have wins as in any battle. In order to win the war we will need to win as many battles as possible.

So where should you begin? I've shared my life lessons as well as ways to improve your mind, body and soul, so what's next? Change is on-going. We need to embrace change, constantly review ourselves, learn to modify in order to keep up with the times and then go back and modify again. Change needs to change constantly in order for us to keep up with the world. Change must be embraced and we need to understand that change is part of our regular routine. So, change is the constant.

As for me, I am still missing that one key vision — what do I want to be when I grow up? That is the one question I have never really been able to answer until now. I see so many things that interest me and I want to be involved with that I never got down to the one question. What is my true passion and what do I want to do with it? I'm not sure I can answer that question just yet. For now, I will focus on my passion for coaching and mentoring other business people.

What's next you may ask? As I say, if nothing changes then nothing will ever change. I guess we'll have to change things up for my next opportunity.

About the Author

Michael Zeidenberg is a seasoned executive with over 35 years of business experience with a focus on leadership. Michael has developed a successful track record of nurturing and growing the financial well-being of a number of family run and corporate companies.

Early on Michael was exposed to the dynamics of how business and family integrate with one another through his family's business in transportation. This sparked a passion that would remain ever present in the roles and clients Michael would take on throughout In his career.

From Strategic Planning to developing Operational and Financial Excellence Michael has created a process that his clients can easily adopt while ensuring they achieve key milestones within their businesses.

Michael continues to offer his services while facilitating a number of training and strategic planning sessions to existing and new clients.

Michael currently resides in Toronto with his wife Marla and together spends time with their kids; Brian, Jordanna and her husband Joey and granddaughter Scarlett.

Michael can be reached at michaelzeidenberg@gmail.com

Printed in Great Britain
by Amazon